S0-BCA-688

TREK THE RAIN FOREST

BY K.C. KELLEY

AMICUS READERS ● AMICUS INK

Amicus Readers and Amicus Ink are imprints of Amicus
P.O. Box 1329, Mankato, MN 56002
www.amicuspublishing.us

Copyright © 2018 Amicus. International copyright reserved in all countries. No part of this book may be reproduced in any form without written permission from the publisher.

Cataloging-in-Publication Data is on file with the Library of Congress.
ISBN 978-1-68151-312-6 (library binding)
ISBN 978-1-68152-268-5 (paperback)
ISBN 978-1-68151-348-5 (eBook)

Editor: Marysa Storm/Megan Peterson
Designer: Patty Kelley
Photo Researcher/Producer: Shoreline Publishing Group LLC

Photo Credits:
Cover: Soft_Light/Adobe Stock Images
Adobe Stock: Jiri Vondrous 16T; Dreamstime.com: Filipe Frazao 5, Papi8888 10, Rafael Ben Ari 16B; Shutterstock: Maridav 3, photoinnovation 6, Kjersti Joergensen 9, Mark Tucan 13, MaeManee 15, Pruit Phatsrivong 16R.

Printed in China.

HC 10 9 8 7 6 5 4 3 2 1
PB 10 9 8 7 6 5 4 3 2 1

Wow! Dana looks at the trees.
Let's explore this rain forest.

Some rain forests
are huge.
The Amazon River
flows through
this one.

A lot of rain falls
in rain forests.
Trees and vines
grow well.
Flowers bloom!

Amazing animals
live in rain forests.
Jackson sees
a monkey.

Not all rain forest animals are big. Bugs fly and crawl in rain forests.

Rain forests
help Earth.
They are home
to lots of life.

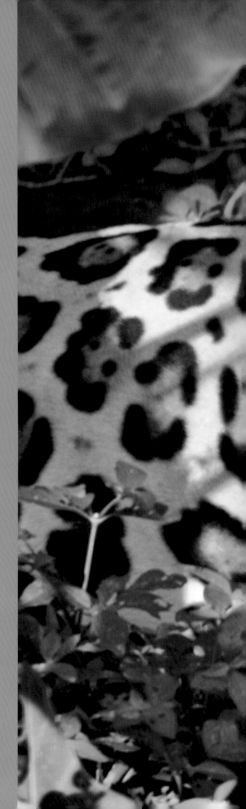

Night is coming.
Kim and her dad
walk home.

RAIN FOREST ANIMALS

parrot

tree snake

pink river
dolphin

16